THE SICKENING HISTORY OF MEDICINE

Strange Medicine

A HISTORY OF MEDICAL REMEDIES

Thanks to the creative team:
Senior Editor: Alice Peebles
Editor: Angela Koo
Fact Checker: Kate Mitchell
Design: www.collaborate.agency

Hungry Tomato™
A division of Lerner Publishing Group, Inc.
241 First Avenue North
Minneapolis, MN 55401 USA

For reading levels and more information, look up this title at
www.lernerbooks.com.

Main body text set in Futura Std Book, 11/14.
Typeface provided by Adobe Systems.

Library of Congress Cataloging-in-Publication Data

Names: Farndon, John. | Dean, Venitia, 1976– illustrator.
Title: Strange medicine : a history of medical remedies/ John
Farndon ; illustrated by Venitia Dean.
Description: Minneapolis : Hungry Tomato, 2017. | Series:
The sickening history of medicine | Audience: Age 8–12. |
Audience: Grade 4 to 6. | Includes index.
Identifiers: LCCN 2016025651 (print) | LCCN 2016026874
(ebook) | ISBN 9781512415599 (lb : alk. paper) | ISBN
9781512430769 (pb : alk. paper) | ISBN 9781512427110 (eb
pdf)
Subjects: LCSH: Medicine—History—Juvenile literature.
| Medicine—Juvenile literature. | Alternative medicine—
Juvenile literature. | Traditional medicine—Juvenile
literature.
Classification: LCC R133.5 .F37 2017 (print) | LCC R133.5
(ebook) | DDC 610—dc23

LC record available at https://lccn.loc.gov/2016025651

Manufactured in the United States of America
1-39919-21389-8/16/2016

THE SICKENING
HISTORY OF MEDICINE

Strange
Medicine

By John Farndon

Illustrated by Venitia Dean

HUNGRY
TOMATO

Contents

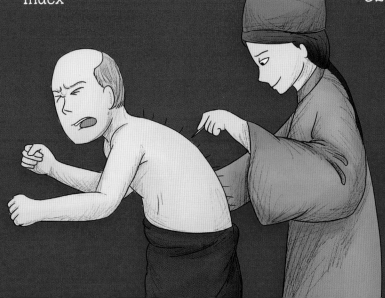

INTRODUCTION

When someone gets sick, they need the right medicine to help them get better. But just what is the right medicine? That's a problem that has been plaguing doctors since ancient times. Throughout history, doctors have come up with some really great ideas for healing people—but also some very, very bad ones . . .

Germ Killers

Some medicines are designed to help people get better by fighting infections. Antibiotics, for example, are medicines that kill or attack the germs that make people ill. Antibiotics only work against bacteria. To fight viruses, you need special antiviral drugs.

Correcting Mistakes

Sometimes the body makes too much or too little of certain chemicals. Some medicines are designed to replace missing chemicals or block their production when the body is making too much. Diabetics, for example, are given insulin (which used to be taken from the pancreases of pigs) to replace the insulin their bodies are unable to make.

Soothing the Symptoms

Some medicines are not meant to cure people—they are just designed to make them feel better by relieving the symptoms. For example, pain relievers can make headaches or sore throats less painful. And creams can make skin less itchy.

Medical Business

Americans use as much medicine as the rest of the world put together. Every year, they buy and use a third of a trillion dollars' worth of medicines! In other words, every single American uses one thousand dollars' worth of drugs every year. So they must be very well, or very sick . . .

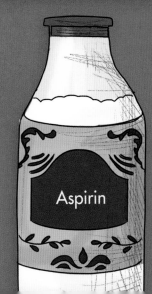

Aspirin

ANCIENT MEDICINE

Many herbs and natural materials have healing properties. But people learned long ago that these natural medicines can often be made more effective by preparing or mixing them in certain ways. This ancient art of pharmacy dates back to Ancient Egypt and beyond.

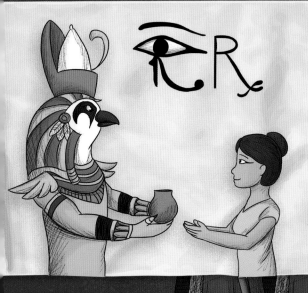

The Father of Pharmacy

The Ancient Egyptians believed pharmacy began with the god Horus. Horus lost his eye in battle, but it was healed by the god Thoth. Modern pharmacists write "Rx" on prescriptions for medicine. Some believe they are writing the ancient sign for the eye of Horus. Others think that Rx is just medieval shorthand for the Latin for "recipe."

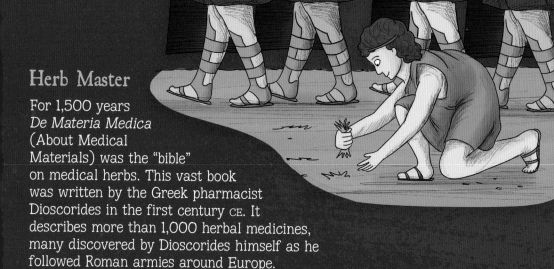

Herb Master

For 1,500 years *De Materia Medica* (About Medical Materials) was the "bible" on medical herbs. This vast book was written by the Greek pharmacist Dioscorides in the first century CE. It describes more than 1,000 herbal medicines, many discovered by Dioscorides himself as he followed Roman armies around Europe.

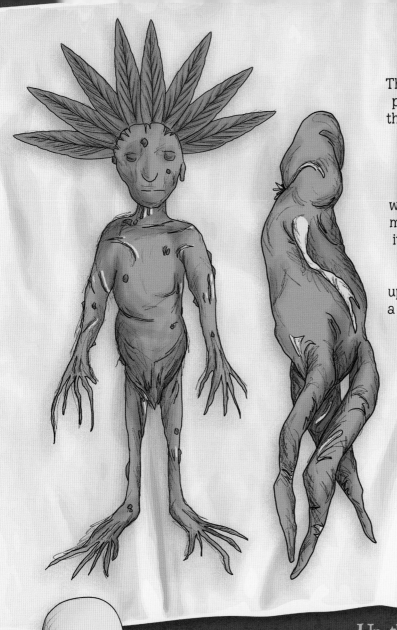

Screaming Root

The root of the mandrake plant is a powerful drug that causes hallucinations and sends people to sleep. The roots can be shaped like a little person, and the plant was long thought to have magic powers. Some said it screamed when pulled from the ground and cursed the person who uprooted it, so people tied a poor dog to the plant to pull it up instead.

Up the Back

We take most drugs through our mouths, but long ago some doctors had the idea of putting them into the body from the other end. Basically, they stuck a tube called a clyster pipe into the patient's bottom. Then they attached a tube to squirt the medicine in. Modern doctors still use this method, only they call it an *enema*.

9

CHINESE ROOTS

The Chinese have an ancient tradition of looking for cures in nature. But they don't just use herbs for medicine—they have used all kinds of other strange things too, from scorpion stings to centipedes.

Live Forever!

For many centuries, Chinese chemists searched for a pill that would make people live forever. One story tells of a man called Wei Bo-yang who did succeed in making an immortality pill. The story also says that the legendary Yellow Emperor found this pill and lived on forever.

The Point of Medicine

Acupuncture involves sticking sharp needles into the skin. The needles activate healing pathways, or meridians, in the body. Acupuncture has been practiced in China for 2,000 years, and it may have been known in Europe long ago too. Ötzi, a man from 5,000 years ago who was found frozen in mountain ice, had tattoos that seemed to mark acupuncture meridians.

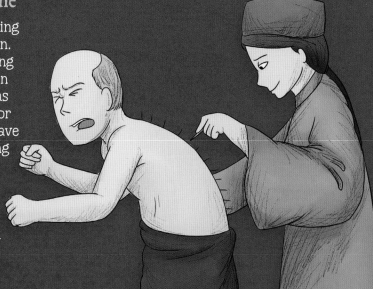

This Medicine Stings!

Most of us would steer clear of scorpions. The sting in their tail is always painful and can be deadly. Yet the Chinese have long believed that pickled scorpions, or *quan xie*, can cure seizures, headaches, and swelling. But maybe patients just said, "I'm better!" as soon as they saw the medicine they were being given!

Snake Wine

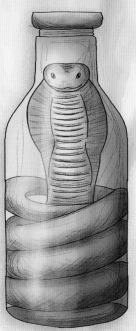

If you're feeling a little tired, or you're losing your hair, what you need is snake wine, according to ancient Chinese medicine. Snake wine is made by drowning a venomous snake in rice wine! It was first used 2,700 years ago.

Killing Seahorses

Seahorses are beautiful marine creatures that are in danger of extinction. Yet those who believe in traditional Chinese medicine buy 25 million of them every year. They are convinced that dried seahorses can cure wheezing, kidney and stomach problems, and much more. But there is no scientific evidence for this.

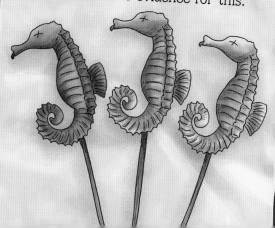

Dragon Bones

The fossilized bones of long-dead creatures are often called dragon bones in China. Ground to a powder, they are used in Chinese medicine to cure heart problems, stress, and fever. In the ancient past, dragon bones, or "oracle bones," were also scratched with questions that people wanted to ask the gods.

IT'S CHEMISTRY

Most modern medicines are made from chemicals rather than herbs, and we owe this to the scientists of Ancient Islam. It all started with the brilliant Jabir ibn Hayyan, also known as Geber, who may have lived in Kufa (in modern Iraq) 1,300 years ago.

Bedside Manner

To get just the right mix of chemicals to make the medicine, Islamic physicians believed they needed to spend time with each patient and find out all they could about their symptoms and character.

Take your Poison

Jabir knew all there was to know at that time about the chemistry of poisons. In his famous *Book of Poisons*, he described hundreds of toxic substances and how they react in the body. He also described antidotes—substances that work against the effects of poison—and gave practical demonstrations of them in action.

Going to the Chemist

Ancient Islamic cities such as Baghdad were packed with pharmacies, all stocked with jars of colorful mixtures of chemicals. We are used to treating illnesses with drugs—that is, substances that affect the chemistry of the body. But back then it was exciting and new.

Poison, Madam?

Many medicines included deadly poisons such as henbane, hemlock, and black nightshade. Ancient chemists weren't trying to kill the sick. In fact, they'd made a crucial discovery: what matters with giving medicines is the dose. In small doses, some poisons are powerful drugs for relieving pain or sending you to sleep. But they didn't always get the dose right. Bye bye!

13

PLUCKED OWLS AND ROAST KITTENS

In the Middle Ages, only the very, very rich had a doctor. If you were ill, you went to the apothecary. Apothecaries were like today's pharmacists. They not only told you what was wrong with you—they prepared their own medicines.

Secret Recipes

Apothecary shops were packed with all kinds of mysterious jars and weird ingredients. Apothecaries liked to keep recipes secret, so some ingredients may have been deliberately misleading. All the same, you might find plucked and boiled owl (for gout), hedgehog grease (for a throat infection), snail slime (for burns), and roast kittens (for jaundice).

Medical Mix

To make a medicine, the apothecary weighed out his chosen ingredients on scales. He ground dry ingredients to a powder in a sturdy bowl called a mortar with a stick called a pestle. He purified and concentrated liquids in a kind of kettle known as an alembic.

Ear This

It seems everything that falls off your body could be mixed into a medicine—hair, fingernails, saliva, old bits of skin . . . If you suffered from bad headaches, some apothecaries would recommend a nice mixture of earwax and mud, usually applied as a balm.

Poo or Pee?

Some apothecaries' cures were awful. If you had a sore throat, some would mix you a nice spoonful of monkey or baby poop with a dollop of honey. If you suffered back pain, they might mix a cup of pee with ox bile, herbs, and suet. And for a fever, you might have to sip pig pee . . .

GREEN MEDICINE

The chemicals and exotic ingredients used by apothecaries were hard to come by or very expensive. So for centuries most people relied on herbs for their medicine. These could be picked from the wild or grown in gardens.

Hildegard's Herbs

One of the most famous books on herbal medicine was written by a twelfth-century German nun, Hildegard of Bingen, who also happened to be one of the first known musical composers. Hildegard believed in "green power," using plants and herbs to cure illnesses. Her books are still referred to today.

Garden of Medicine

Monasteries set up gardens for growing herbs to treat the sick and provide food flavoring and dyes. There were different areas for plants to treat coughs and colds, liver and bladder complaints, digestion, headaches, anxiety and depression, and others.

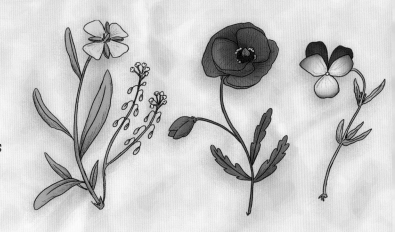

Powerful Burdock

A man named Nicholas Culpeper wrote one of the best books on herbal medicine in 1653. But even Culpeper had some odd ideas. He thought that the herb burdock would prevent farting and rabies and also cure snake bites. He even thought that if women wore it on their heads, it would stop their wombs from collapsing . . .

Lookalikes

It was hard to know which substances would heal which ailments. Many people believed in the "doctrine of signatures." This was the idea that plants and foods could treat the parts of the body that they look like. So since a sliced mushroom looks like an ear, it must be good for hearing.

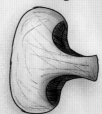

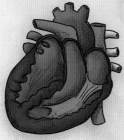

Slice of tomato—
for the heart

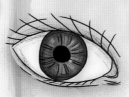

Slice of carrot—for
the eyes

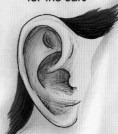

Slice of mushroom—
for the ears

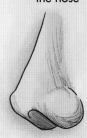

Whole carrot—for
the nose

Wise Woman

In many country villages, if someone was ill, they went to see the witch, who knew all about herbs. For some people, a witch was just a wise old woman who knew how to heal the sick. But other people were afraid of witches' skill and believed witches served the devil.

WILLOW POWER

If someone has a bad headache or another pain, it's easy for them to take an aspirin or another painkiller. But it wasn't always that way . . .

Barking Mad

Aspirin is made from the chemical salicin. A form of salicin occurs naturally in the bark of willow trees, myrtle, and meadowsweet plants. But getting it out of a tree is a real headache . . .

Taming the Snake

Ague (probably malaria) was so nasty that people pictured it as a snake gripping you so you could be attacked by the monster fever! Chewing on Peruvian bark helped, but this wasn't easy to get in England. Then in 1758, Oxfordshire vicar Edward Stone noticed that willow bark tasted a bit like Peruvian bark. He tried it on a few ague victims, and they felt better at once.

Drugged Up

In the 1800s, if someone was in pain, doctors would prescribe a glass of laudanum. This certainly eased the pain, but it was a strong, addictive drug related to heroin. Many who took it became addicted, including many women who took it simply to ease cramps.

Aspirin

The pain-relieving ingredient in willow bark is a chemical called salicin. But salicin is acidic and attacks the stomach. In the 1890s, Bayer company scientists made the wonder drug aspirin by modifying salicin to make it less damaging. No pain, big gain.

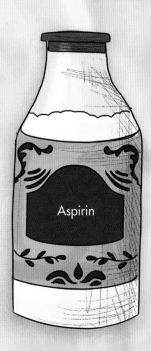

Aspirin

FINDING A MAGIC BULLET

Syphilis is a terrible disease that once ravaged Europe. There seemed to be no cure—until a German physician found a chemical that killed the germs but left the patient unharmed. For him, it was like a magic bullet that killed only the bad.

We've Won!

French king Charles VIII was rather pleased when he marched his conquering army into Naples in Italy in 1495. But his soldiers caught the horrific disease syphilis in the city and spread it across Europe.

Nose Job

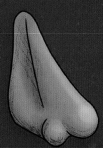

Syphilis didn't often kill people right away, but its effects were really horrible. It made the body burst out with boils so foul that syphilis came to be known as the Great Pox. And it rotted away the nose, so that many syphilis victims had to have artificial noses.

Fume it Out

People were so desperate to be cured of syphilis that they tried anything. The metal mercury was thought to help, and one idea was to sit in a box filled with mercury fumes. But mercury is poisonous, and its effects were painful, unpleasant, and even deadly.

The Deaf Composer

The brilliant composer Ludwig van Beethoven (1770–1827) famously went deaf as he got older, so it became very hard for him to write music. People have wondered if his deafness was caused by syphilis. Other syphilis victims from history include Henry VIII, Adolf Hitler, and the Russian writer Leo Tolstoy.

On Target

The German scientist Paul Ehrlich (1854–1915) believed that if bacteria could be stained colors by certain dyes, then they might also be killed by them, as if by magic bullets. He and his colleagues tried hundreds of stains, and in 1914 they found one that worked against syphilis germs. They used it to make the drug Salvarsan, the first effective treatment for the disease.

21

MOLDY BUT DEADLY

Food that's gone moldy looks pretty yucky, and you wouldn't want to eat it. But it was in mold that Scottish scientist Alexander Fleming discovered the amazing medicine penicillin.

Nasty Staphy

The bacterium *Staphylococcus aureus* is among the world's most common germs. One in five people around the world carries it in their skin and up their nose. It doesn't always make people ill, but when it does, it's nasty. Meningitis, pneumonia, osteomyelitis (a bone disease), flu, boils, and much more are all due to *S. aureus*!

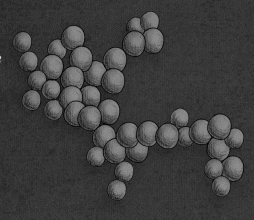

Mold Mayhem

In 1928, Fleming went away on vacation while studying *S. aureus* germs in dishes in his laboratory. When he came back, some dishes had gone moldy. Then he spotted that germs had died where the mold had grown—and he realized the mold contained a natural germ-killing substance, which he called penicillin.

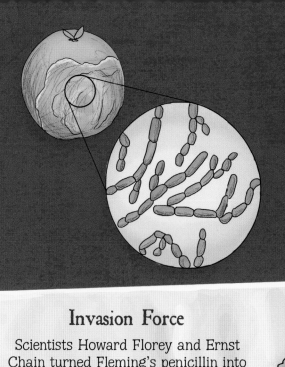

What is Penicillin?

The *Penicillium rubens* mold, in which Fleming found penicillin, belongs to a group of fungi. Like all molds, it grows in tiny threads called hyphae and spreads through the air in minute spores (like seeds). The green fur on a moldy orange is *P. digitatum*. The blue veins in blue cheese are *P. roqueforti*.

Invasion Force

Scientists Howard Florey and Ernst Chain turned Fleming's penicillin into a medicine that would save thousands of lives. They found how to make it in large quantities so it could be used to treat infected wounds. This saved the lives of countless soldiers injured in the D-Day landings of 1944 during World War II.

NATURAL KILLERS

Since Fleming discovered penicillin, scientists have discovered 150 other antibiotics—drugs that attack bacteria. Most antibiotics are entirely man-made. But many were originally found, like penicillin, in natural sources. The antibiotics tetracycline and streptomycin both came from bacteria. And the natural world is full of antibiotic substances that may inspire new drugs. Here are some of the weirdest places that scientists are looking . . .

Alligator Blood

Scientists were baffled that alligators seem to get badly wounded in fights with other alligators, yet their wounds don't become infected. When they investigated, they found that alligator blood contains natural antibiotics effective against a wide range of infections.

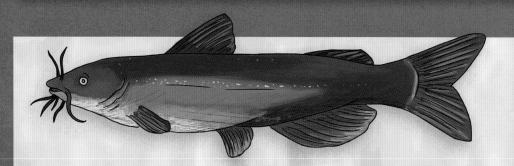

Catfish Slime

Catfish seem to survive injuries without getting infected, and scientists recently found out why. Their bodies are covered in a kind of slime rich in antibiotics that seem to be good at killing off germs such as *Klebsiella pneumoniae*, which attacks the lungs, and *E. coli*.

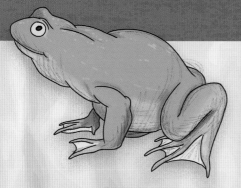

Frog Skin

Frogs can survive in water that would kill other creatures. Scientists know one reason why: their skin is covered in one hundred bacteria-killing substances. Most are also dangerous to humans, so scientists must find a way to apply their powers without hurting us!

Panda Blood

One of the most powerful of all antibiotics, cathelicidin-AM, occurs in panda blood. It kills off germs in a fraction of the time it takes most other antibiotics. But pandas are very rare, so scientists make synthetic panda blood to conduct experiments with cathelicidin-AM.

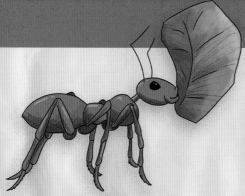

Leafcutter Ants

Leafcutter ants are known for their superstrength in carrying leaves, but they also have superpowers against germs. Scientists have found that their bodies deploy multiple chemicals to fight bacteria and fungi, just as doctors use multi-drug approaches to treat difficult infections.

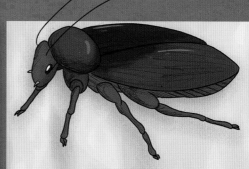

Cockroach Brains

Crushed cockroach brains contain nine different kinds of antibiotic. Scientists are trying to find out if some may be used to treat *E. coli* infections or even MRSA, infection by the *S. aureus* "superbug" bacterium that has become resistant to other antibiotics.

SUGAR IN THE BLOOD

People who have diabetes can't keep down the sugar levels in their blood. The problem lies with the body chemical insulin, which should control sugar levels but doesn't. That's why diabetics—people with diabetes—must receive regular injections of insulin.

Sweet Pees

In the Middle Ages, many doctors knew just how to diagnose diabetes. They tasted the patient's urine. If it tasted sweet, the patient had diabetes. But doctors didn't really know how to treat the disease. Some suggested drinking wine, some recommended eating a lot of sour food, and others said riding horses would do the trick!

Finding Insulin

In 1889, German scientists Oscar Minkowski and Joseph von Mering removed a dog's pancreas for their studies of digestion. Later they saw flies feeding on the dog's pee, found it was sweet, and realized that it is the pancreas that controls sugar levels. In 1921, Canadian Frederick Banting and American Charles H. Best discovered that it does this by making insulin.

Bacteria Factory

In the 1970s, scientists found how to use bacteria as factories for making human insulin. They inserted the gene for human insulin into *E. coli* bacteria, then put them in a huge vat to multiply. As they multiplied, the bacteria followed their new genes' instructions and made lots of human insulin. This is now the main source of insulin for diabetics.

Sweet Swine

The discovery of insulin was a major breakthrough for the treatment of diabetes. Insulin could be taken from the pancreases of pigs and cows killed for meat. Then it was refined and given to diabetics in injections that kept their condition under control.

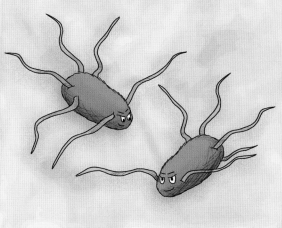

Out of the Box

Pandora was a mythical girl who was so curious that she opened a box and let out things that would hurt mankind, such as war and disease. Some scientists were worried that genetically modified bacteria for making insulin might escape and spread— just like opening Pandora's box. At a conference in 1975, they agreed they should never work with disease-causing bacteria and should always work in a completely secure room.

MEDICINE THROUGH TIME

Medicines have come a long way from the simple herbs used in ancient times to the mass-produced chemical drugs of today. Here are some milestones in their development.

About 1520 Dose

Swiss-German scholar Paracelsus was a bit of an odd guy who liked creating mysteries, but he established that medicines (and poisons) must be given in the right doses to have the right effects.

1000 BCE

1000 CE

About 2500 BCE
Divine Farmer-cy

Shennong, also known as the Divine Farmer, was a mythical ruler of China who tested the medical effects of hundreds of herbs and laid the foundations for Chinese traditional medicine still followed today.

About 800 CE
Poison King

Persian chemist Jabir ibn Hayyan wrote the first great book on the chemistry of medicines, *Book of Poisons*.

About 60 CE Medical Material

The Greek-born Roman physician Dioscorides wrote a five-volume guide to the medical effects of herbs and other substances, called *De Materia Medica* (On Medical Material).

1897 Counter Pain

The Bayer chemical company introduced aspirin, the first widely sold everyday painkilling medicine.

1910 Magic Bullet

Salvarsan was the first magic bullet drug, designed to target the bacteria that cause disease. It was the first effective treatment for syphilis.

1921 Sweet Discovery

Frederick Banting, Charles Best, and John Macleod discovered insulin—the chemical produced by the pancreas that controls levels of sugar in the blood—and that diabetes could be treated with injections of artificial insulin.

1800   2000

1870 Clean Surgery

Surgeon Joseph Lister showed how keeping everything completely clean cut the chances of germs spreading and killing patients undergoing surgery.

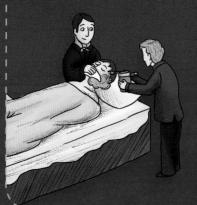

1928 Medicine from Mold

Scottish doctor Alexander Fleming discovered penicillin, the first known natural bacteria killer, or antibiotic, in mold.

1948 Sore Losers

Corticosteroid drugs, discovered by Edward Kendall and Philip Hinch, reduce inflammation, which is a key symptom of ailments such as rheumatism.

THE RIGHT PRESCRIPTION

For headaches and low spirits, medieval herbalists gave concoctions including the herbs betony and vervain. Modern scientists have discovered that both of these contain chemicals good for treating migraines and depression.

According to one ancient papyrus, the Ancient Egyptians used donkey, dog, gazelle, and fly dung as medicine, taken through the mouth.

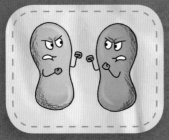

Since the discovery of antibiotics, more and more bacteria have developed resistance to them, mostly through overuse.

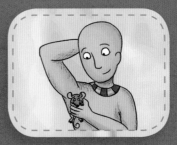

The Ancient Egyptians used lizard blood, dead mice, mud, and moldy bread as ointments for sores.

According to legend, the Ancient Greek king Mithridates developed an antidote to all poisons. The Romans turned it into theriac, a drug that would cure all ailments. It didn't work, but people continued using it until the late 1800s.

Recently, scientists tested a medieval eye cure made from onions, garlic, wine, and a bull's gall bladder juice. It looked yucky but had amazing antibacterial properties.

GLOSSARY

acupuncture	an ancient Chinese treatment involving inserting needles into the body
alembic	a kind of kettle with a long spout, used by apothecaries for purifying liquids
antibiotic	a drug that attacks bacteria
apothecary	someone who mixed and sold medicines
bacterium	a very small living thing made from just a single living cell. A small number of them cause disease. *Bacteria* is the plural of *bacterium*.
clyster pipe	a pipe for injecting fluids and gases up a patient's rear end for medical purposes
doctrine of signatures	the idea that treatments for different parts of the body can be identified by similar shapes in nature
immortality	living forever
insulin	the body chemical that regulates levels of sugar in the blood
laudanum	an addictive painkilling drink made by mixing the drug opium in alcohol
mortar	a bowl used by apothecaries for grinding and mixing medicines
penicillin	a substance in the *Penicillium* mold that kills bacteria
pestle	a stick used by apothecaries for grinding medicine to a powder in a mortar
salicin	a substance found in meadowsweet and the bark of willow trees that is used to reduce inflammation and to make aspirin

Index

The Author

John Farndon is the author of many books on science, technology, and nature, including the international best sellers *Do Not Open* and *Do You Think You're Clever?* He has been shortlisted six times for the Royal Society's Young People's Book Prize for a science book.

The Illustrator

Venitia Dean grew up in Brighton, in the United Kingdom. She has loved drawing ever since she could hold a pencil. After receiving a digital drawing tablet for her nineteenth birthday, she began working digitally. She hasn't looked back since!